ECONOMIC DISPARITIES AND FISCAL CORRECTIVES IN FEDERAL COUNTRIES

ECONOMIC DISPARITIES AND FISCAL CORRECTIVES IN FEDERAL COUNTRIES

India, Canada and Australia

Gargi Sengupta

GenNext Publication

ISBN : 978-93-8022-237-0

Price : ₹ 90

First Published, 2016

Published by

Gennext Publications
5, Ansari Road
Daryaganj, New Delhi-110002
Phones: 9811692060
E-mail: gennext@hotmail.com

Printed at: G. Print Process, Delhi.

Cataloging in Publication Data—DK
Courtesy: D.K. Agencies (P) Ltd. <docinfo@dkagencies.com>

Sengupta, Gargi.
Economic disparities and fiscal correctives in federal countries : India, Canada and Australia / Gargi Sengupta.
p. cm.
Includes bibliographical references (p.).
ISBN 9789380222370

1. Intergovernmental fiscal relations—India. 2. Intergovernmental fiscal relations—Canada. 3. Intergovernmental fiscal relations—Australia. 4. Fiscal policy—India. 5. Fiscal policy—Canada. 6. Fiscal policy—Australia. I. Title.

DDC 336.54 23

Contents

Preface

India is a Union of States. In practice India has acted like a federal country by its way of putting federalism in governance structure and in relationship between the Union Government and the State Governments.

Since the Constitution of India has drawn inputs largely from Constitution of different countries, it is therefore necessary to know from which country or countries India had adopted the model of federalism. Thus in this book I made an attempt to compare the federal structure of India with that of the federal structure of Canada and Australia.

The process of federalism remains incomplete if it is limited only up to the division of political powers because for running the administration of the country, economic powers are equally important. This urge for economic power leads to the concept of fiscal federalism.

During my Post Graduation days in JNU, I had the opportunity of preparing a paper on federalism, which I feel is quite relevant in the present context, when the entire country and the world are the supporters of the concept of participation and inclusion in governance structure. It is in this background, in this book I discussed the concept of federalism in general and fiscal federalism in particular, to show that unless fiscal federalism is practiced in the country, the prospect of survival of political federalism gets reduced.

Acknowledgements

First I would like to convey my gratitude to Prof. Balveer Arora, my guide during M.A. Research Course, for his suggestions and guidance during the course of this study. He led me to various dimensions and perspectives of this subject which helped me throughout the journey of this study.

I am thankful to Centre for Political Studies, School of Social Sciences, Jawaharlal Nehru University, the Central Library and the SAP Library for their support and cooperation at every stage of my work.

I would also like to thank my husband, family, friends and well wishers for their constant encouragement and motivation in completion of the book.

Gargi Sengupta

Introduction

In the modern era of multi-tired governance, a new way of protecting liberty and improving governance is the process of federalism. Federalism is not only about division of political powers and authorities between one central and the State governments, but it also has an economic perspective of its own. The economic factors have played an important role in the evolution of federalism in the twentieth century unless there is economic parity and stability present between various levels of governments as the political federalism doesn't survive long.[1]

Further the concept of shared-rule under federalism has an implicit acknowledgment for having both political and economic relations between the Central and the State governments.[2]

Thus, in federalism, parity is achieved through the exercise of powers in such a way that it protects and preserves the separate diversities of the units. Because of this inter-linkages present between the political and economic spheres of federalism, it is very important to have an outlook of this beyond the so-called political framework. It has been enunciated by the economist that the theory of fiscal federalism represents a polar case where fiscal arrangements are decided purely on the basis of economic principles.[3]

As we know in reality that such ideal situations can never be achieved. This particular view point has been elaborated by M. Govinda Rao. According to him, "economists tend to view federalism somewhat different from political scientists. Their concern is not only with equity but with efficiency."[4]

Therefore, economics of multi-level governing systems help us to understand *inter-alia* of three vital aspects:

1. Optimal degree of fiscal decentralisation;
2. Assignments of functions and finances to different levels of government;
3. Establish a coordination in tax and expenditure required that is,
   (a) To design suitable inter governmental transfer, and
   (b) To improving inter jurisdictional interactions.

Thus, the principles of fiscal federalism through an economic angle tries to find purely economic solutions to federal problems. However, historical, social and political factors also play an important role in the consideration of economic efficiency. Therefore, the influence of non-economic factors on federal fiscal arrangements places a constraint on the efficiency of purely economic solutions in solving federal fiscal problems. But viewed from a different ground level perspectives, where "economic disparities", "social disparities" and "political disparities" persist in ample measures, then for the very survival of federalism, fiscal federalism requires those fiscal correctives which apart from meeting some economic criteria must address the economic and social concerns arising out of disparities in those spheres.

In this context my primary objective is getting a clear view on the concept of fiscal federalism. I have tried to explore why fiscal allocation is one of the major typologies of any federations. For easy understanding I have divided my work into three chapters. The first chapter will define the concept of fiscal federalism. The second chapter, primarily deals with Indian case study, where I explain the notion of economic disparity and what should be the possible measures that are to be taken to address these disparities in view of finding an ever-lasting solution. Third chapter explores a comparative study of Indian fiscal federalism with Canadian and the Australian fiscal federalism, and finally the Conclusion.

References

1. Ajit Mazumdar, *The Political Economy of Federalism,* in B. Arora and Varney (eds.), Multiple Identities in a Single State, ch-7, pp. 197—233.
2. See more details in *Ibid.,* pp. 240—444.
3. M.G. Rao, *India's Fiscal Federalism from a Comparative Perspectives,* in B. Arora and D.V. Verney (eds.) Indian Federalism in Comparative Perspectives, pp. 272—316.
4. *Ibid.,* p. 273.

1 The Concept of Fiscal Federalism

Michael Burgess (2006)[1] says, "federalism is the animating force of federation and it can take many different forms: historical, intellectual, cultural, ideological, social, economic, territorial, non territorial, etc." Therefore federalism is a multi-dimensional concept. The issue of fiscal federalism is one of the most important dimensions of federalism. It being the most crucial typology of federalism the fiscal federalism has significant value as it solely determines the allocation of finance for the Central as well as for the State Governments.

Federalism is not only about political federalism in which a group of members are assigned to do a specific jobs in their respective fields. This political federalism has no meaning unless there is fiscal federalism because political freedom and decentralisation cannot be achieved in a sustainable way, if there is no financial freedom and decentralisation available for the States—as no state can survive without finance. Therefore, we need to have not only federalism as a standalone arrangement but also fiscal federalism must go hand in hand with it so that the finances are shared by both the Central, State, and local governments in a harmonious and meticulous way facilitating both horizontal and vertical mobility and growth amongst the units forming the federation.

The issue of 'fiscal federalism' is basically about sharing the costs of running a federal country and what sort of federal makeup is best, suited to the economic parameters of federal countries. Therefore, fiscal federalism is a system of transfer of payments or grants by which a federal government shares its revenues with lower level of governments. Federal governments follow two primary types of transfers:

(i) *Conditional*: A conditional transfer from a federal body to a province or territories, which involves certain conditions that is, if a lower level of government wants to receive this type of transfer, it must agree to the spending instructions of the federal government.

(ii) *Unconditional*: Unconditional transfer is about a cash without instructions transfer.

The federal government is designed for specific limited powers with most basic government functions are left to the states.[2] That is why fiscal division is very important so that both the governments have financial powers and resources to carry forward their respective works. And the best way of fiscal division is to have a decentralised fiscal system. It explores more avenues for improving the macro-economic governance, than the centralised fiscal system exeutes. Decentralised fiscal system requires greater clarity about the roles of various players and decision-makers to ensure a fair play of greater transparency in roles governing interaction. So, a decentralised fiscal federal structure offers economics of scale for both national level public goods and it also accommodates diversity of preference at the sub-national level.

Fiscal decentralisation involves transferring expenditure and revenue responsibilities from the Central Government to subnational governments. The degree of decentralisation can be measured by the extent the sub-national governments enjoy the autonomy *vis-a-vis* the Central government. The most important point is that this "autonomy" should include fiscal autonomy also; it is the financial resource which is required to meet the needs for good governance.

The design of any fiscal federal relation therefore includes "expenditure assignment, revenue assignment, inter-governmental transfer, tax administration, budgeting and financial management in a multi-level governmental setting.[3] This particular outlook of federal system, properly functions under a decentralised administration because it would ensure greater responsibility and accountability of the subnational authorities for the performance of taxes assigned to them, as well as greater flexibility in adapting systems and procedures to local need and conditions. That means fiscal federalism assigns functions to different tiers/ orders/levels of governments on one hand and on the other side, it also provides fiscal instruments for carrying out these functions. So the decentralised model is intended to conform that model in which powers and funds are transferred from higher-level institutions to the state local-level institutions.[4] This form of transfer may include powers of decision-making (administrative decentralisation) arid also sometimes powers to raise revenues (fiscal decentralisation).

As per these discussions on fiscal federalism and fiscal decentralisation, one can easily say that there is a close connection between the two concepts.[5] Fiscal federalism constitutes a set of guiding principles, a guiding concept, that helps in designing the financial relation between, the national and sub national levels of government and fiscal decentralisation, on the other hand, is a process of applying such principles. Therefore the first concept is more theoratical and the second one is of more practical use, respectively. So the point is that unless there is a balance between the theoretical part and the practical process, it is very difficult to manage the entire conception of federalism—thus there are certain basic principles, on which the concept of fiscal decentralisation works. These principals are bound to be transparent and efficient in nature so that they can enhance the interaction between central and state (in some cases, even in the local levels) governments.[6] They are as follows:

1. Each level of governments should have constitutionally assigned responsibilities to them, so that overlaps are avoided and there should be a

"concurrent list" where all the tires of government can share their responsibilities with each other.

2. As federal process is characterised by non-centralisation, therefore there should be multiple centers of political decisions making. Because of this "non-centralised" governing mechanism neither the central government nor the constituent governments can unilaterally alter the governing mechanism and arrangements.

3. Fiscal equalisation should be brought out in policies and strategies, within the functioning of a federal system of governments so to, mainly, reduce the fiscal disparities among regional jurisdictions. Fiscal equalisation means redistribution of revenues in order to ensure that all constituent units can have equal level of services at comparable costs (tax).[7]

4. Central Government should increase the incentives of the subnational states, so that the sub-national states can work efficiently.

5. The sub-national states should have sound estimate of resources because as deficient in fiscal control may disturb the state programmes due to lack of expenditure.

6. Certain fiscal institutional disciplines should be observed by both Central and the state governments.

   For example:

   to have a balance operating budgets,

   to have a state expenditure authority,

   to have a state revenue raising authority, and

   to have a transparent national transfer policies relating to states etc.

The Issue of Fiscal Sovereignty and Autonomy

As the state and provincial governments face "negative fiscal shock", they do not have any other viable alternative other than either to allow fiscal adjustments and endure political pain on its own or to face unsustainable debt path and then ask Central Government for an unplanned debt relief transfer (*i.e.,* fiscal decisions are more or less based on the guidelines of Central Government.)[8] To avoid the negative shocks and unsustainable deficits, the state and provincial governments demand "fiscal sovereignty and autonomy" for the fulfillment of their economic needs and requirements. As the arrangements of raising, sharing and spending of money is important (for both economic and political purpose), when the states and provinces are facing unexpected fiscal deficits and financial constraints, they refuse to introduce new taxes or adjustments and new financial rules imposed by the Central Government. Rather, the state and provincial governments want to reshape their fiscal sovereignty so that the basic structure of inter governmental fiscal relations between higher and lower level governments improve.[9]

According to Jonathan Rodden, the concept of fiscal sovereignty and autonomy is possible only under decentralised fiscal system. Decentralised fiscal system is quite sensible towards the economic arrangements, which determine and collect taxes and revenues. The decentralised federalism is primarily talking about the real financial division in a federal system where both the Central and the State Governments are sovereign and autonomous in their respective areas of functioning.

The term federal finance means the aggregate fiscal activities of the Central, State and local governments and the relationship between them. Therefore federal finance is multi level finance and the financial authorities of each level of governance are mutually exclusive[10] (except in some cases as per the laws of the constitution). Thus in a federalism at least two constitutionally independent fiscal system operate upon the resources of the individual. That means, the fiscal and monetary position of a government not only decides its position *vis-a-vis* the other government, rather fiscal/ monetary powers but also decide how much a government can establish or control the people of its respective area.

So, fiscal balance between the various tiers of governments is an important concern of a federal system. It has been noticed that the states/local governments want autonomy in political-territorial terms[11] that is an arrangement that grants to a group a means to express its distinct identity, rather they (state and local governments) want "fiscal autonomy" that is increasing the financial position of the state and local governments *vis-a-vis* the center. The main justification given by the subnational states for fiscal autonomy is that in most cases, the authority over taxation has remained centralised and even the center maintains an active role in inter-regional redistribution and regulation of sub-national finances. Therefore in a multi-tired system, "fiscal management" is needed the most, and this is possible if we club the two processes, *i.e.*, fiscal decentralisation and federal decentralisation, so that all the levels of governments get the opportunity to have "sovereignty and autonomy" not only in political terms but also in financial federal forms.[12] And for financial federal sovereignty and autonomy, there is a need for redistribution of macro—economic stability.

Fiscal Decentralisation and Federal Decentralisation: Is it a Two-way Process?

According to Akhtar Majeed, through decentralisation, fiscal federalism becomes more economically efficient process, as it links "those who pay with those who decide and those who benefits." Therefore federal decentralisation and fiscal decentralisation ensure a balance between independence and inter-dependence of governments.

The failure of the centralised state both in economic and in political governance, has shifted the focus in the favour of a decentralised system. As a decentralised system helps to enhance efficiency and minimise transaction costs in the provision of service and ensure greater participation of the people in the decision-making process.[13]Fiscal federalism is the mainstream literature of decentralisation as it broadens the concept of fiscal federalism. And more over, decentralisation combines the political and economic element of federalism which ultimately help the multi-level governmental units to get assigned with both political and fiscal powers. This shows that federal decentralisation inspite of being a political factor, influences and affects the functioning of fiscal federalism (economic factor).[14]

M Govinda Rao and Nirvinkar Singh (2005) bring the concept of political economy of federalism in the context of the relationship between federal and fiscal decentralisation, according to which, "federalism as a political organisation" work on the principle of division of powers between the Central and State Governments. Both these levels of government have some fixed specific activities on which it can make final decisions. But on the other hand, the economic side of the federalism provides certain types of goods and services, these goods are basically public goods *i.e.,* federalism enters into the realm of public sector activities and decisions.

Fiscal federalism deals with economic decisions-making in federal system of government, in which public sector decisions are taken by various layers of the government. So, economic federalism or fiscal federalism is an area of study in which the principles of economics are applied to the functioning of the public sector, thus fiscal federalism make optional institutional arrangements for the provision of public services. Therefore, the combination of fiscal federalism and decentralisation is advantageous for all levels of governments specially in the matter of division of taxes and expenditure pertaining to public sector activities. Thus, fiscal federalism, to a great extent, joints the autonomous political and economic spheres of activities.[15]

The theory of fiscal federalism is concerned with the division, of public-sector functions and finances, in a logical way among the multiple layers of government, and thus fiscal federalism observes a "decentralised theorem." According to decentralised theorem of fiscal federalism, 'local public goods', 'state public goods' and 'national public goods' all play an important role in defining the beneficiaries of financial provisions.[16] Public sector activities is the foccal point of every government's governance. And through fiscal decentralisation these public sector activities get a primary position as fiscal decentralisation adds a new thinking in public sector in the form of efficiency, effectiveness, responsiveness and political accountability in service delivery. So, "fiscal management" is very important as it is not only a process in itself rather it is the outcome or result of a comprehensive multi-government system, where the objectives and policies of a national, state and local government merge together. Thus, fiscal federalism ensures that public services correspond to the diversified demands of a federation. (Fig. 1.1).

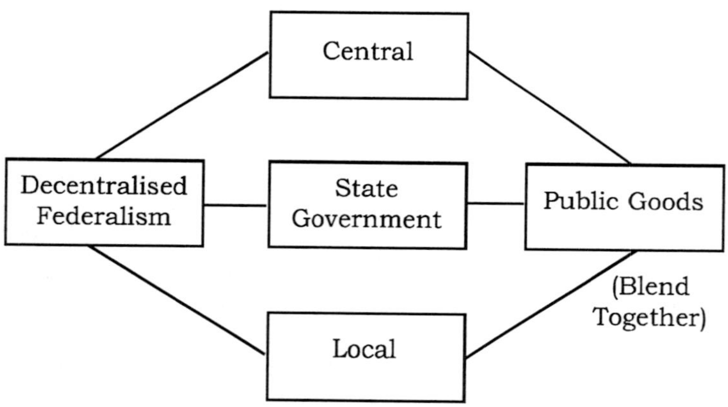

Fig. 1.1. Fiscal Management or Fiscal Balance

Refrences

1. Michael Burgess, *Comparative Federalism: Theory and Practice,* pp. 4—6.
2. See more in www.downsizinggovernment.org/fiscal—federalism.
3. *Fiscal Federalism Manage and Settings between the Central and the State Governments from the View Point of Decentralisation.* Balver Arora and D.V. Varney (eds.), pp. 270—271.
4. India follows the model of democratic decentralisation. p. 5.
5. See more in Chanchal Kumar Sharma, *The Federal Approach to Fiscal Decentralisation: Conceptual, Contours for Policy Makers,* pp. 45—46.
6. *Fiscal Federalism—A Comparative Cross Country Analysis,* www.rbidocs.rbi.org.in/rdocs/Publications/PDFs/74875.
7. Fiscal equalisation is a technique of providing fiscal national unity.
8. The Central Government may or may not committed to the requirement of State finances.
9. J. Rodders, *'On migration of fiscal sovereignty',* political science and politics, Vol. 37, (July, 2004), pp. 427—431.
10. Wallace E. Oates, *'Theory of federalism and economic growth",* the Canadian Journal of Economics, Vol. I, No. (Feb. 1968), pp. 37—54.
11. Autonomy in political – territorial term means – through a group of people have different identity yet they have a space in the majority.
12. Fiscal sovereignty and autonomy is about having supreme authority over the financial matters.
13. Ajit Mazumdar, pp. 9—10.
14. *Ibid.,* p. 6.
15. Under the concept of fiscal federalism the benefits of political autonomous regimes and the benefits of economic consideration combined with each other.
16. M Bird, *Fiscal Federalism,* www.urban.org/uploaded ppdf/1000529.pdf.

2 A Case Study of India

Fiscal autonomy is the most important dimension of federalism as political autonomy is a myth without adequate fiscal autonomy of the federating units. For having a healthy relationship between Center and the States, the later must have something like fiscal autonomy, otherwise the fiscal dependence of the States on the Centre may disturb the entire formats of federation.

Now, the point is what is the actual meaning of fiscal autonomy? Fiscal autonomy can be defined as the exercise of fiscal powers and functions without intervension or direction from another level of governments. Fiscal autonomy largely depends on the amount of revenues government generates to meet the need of its expenditure commitment.[1]

Federal countries in a great deal differs in their choices about the character of fiscal federalism. They want how the division of fiscal power is allocated among various tiers of government is solely dependant upon the fiscal arrangements, which a federal country aspires for. For example, the countries like Brazil, Canada, Switzerland are highly decentralised federations, whereas Australia, Germany, Malaysia etc., are relatively centralised. Even allocation of fiscal power among members are asymmetric, this form federalism is practiced in India.[2] So, what sort of federal make-up best suits to the economic parameters in a give scenario is decided by the federal country itself.

In this particular chapter, main emphasises are given to analyse the fiscal character of Indian federalism. India has a federal form of government and hence a federal financial system. The essence of federalism (i.e., the Center and State Governments should be independent on each other in their respective, constitutionally demarcated sphere of action) get disturbed unless each level of government does not have the adequate resource to discharge its function. India is not an association or confederation of states rather it is a "Union of States" (Article 1 of Constitution) thus, Indian federation is neither the result of an agreement between the units and nor the units have the right to secede from the federation. The point which to be highlighted is that in India the units are neither politically autonomous nor economically. So, to justify that Prof. K.C. Wheare says, "Indian Union is a unitary state with subsidiary federal features rather than a federal state with subsidiary unitary features".

The structuring of Center-state relations is a complex process, as India's federalism started as a system with distinctive centralising features like the office of governor, all India administrative services, center's emergency powers, centralised revenue etc., and these centralised tendency of Indian federalism led to the illustration of over-centralisation especially in financial matters.[3] Due to over-centralisation, financial imbalances develop relating to the powers of taxation assigned to the Union and to the States.

India's Fiscal—Federal System

The constitution of India has specified the responsibilities of spending resources as well as the funds raising domains for the Central and the State governments through three lists: Union List, State List, and the Concurrent List. Similarly, the revenue raising power are also specified. But it faces a serious problem due to asymmetry and economic diversity, there is need to transfer the resources from the Center to the States.

Fiscal system refers to the mechanism through which financial resources for the governments are procured, channeled or raised and the scale and pattern of allocation of such resources is determined.[4] In Indian fiscal system, the budgetary resources and expenditure are determined through the annual budget of the Central and State governments. But still it is the Center who plays the most crucial, and dominant role *vis-a-vis* the States.

Indian, fiscal federalism has evolved within the framework of a Constitution with a high-degree of centripetal basis. So, the basic matrix of the Central, and the State governments are very much confined in terms of the excecuting the powers into the provisions of the Constitution, concerning with the transfer of financial resources from the Center to the States.[5] It is observed by the 6th Finance Commission in 1973 "the heads of revenue and responsibilities were distributed on the basis of whether the Center or the States ware better equipped to deal with the particular head"[6] and the result is, more focused and centralised financial power. An examination of the Central, the State and concurrent lists set out in the 7th schedule to the constitution clearly brings out this mis-match. Like, earlier the union list had 97 subjects, now it has 99, even in the concurrent list from 47 items have increased to 52 items but in the case of state list, it was reduced from 67 subjects to 61. And the residuary power also belongs to the Central government.[7] Thus, all these constitutional provisions make it clear that mostly it is the State governments which have to compromise and negotiate more *vis-a-vis* with the Central government. Be it legislative power, administrative power or the financial power, the state governments have to follow the rules and decisions of the Central Government.

No system of federation can be successful unless both the Central and the States have at their disposal adequate financial resources to enable them to discharge their respective responsibilities under the Constitution. Thus, the needs of proper and systematic distribution of financial resources is very important.[8] The point is that this distribution of financial resources is the prime cause of conflict between the Center and the States. To understand this distribution of financial resources, it is very important to look at the FEDERAL SCHEME of the Indian Constitution.

Centre-state Financial Relations: The Federal Scheme

(a) The Scheme of Distribution of Sources of Revenue[9]

(1) Taxes levied by the Union but collected and appropriated, by the state (Article 268). Example: stamp duties, duties of excise on medicinal, toilet preparation etc.

(2) Taxes levied and collected by the center but assigned to the state (Article 269). For example, succession and estate duties, taxes on railway fares, terminal taxes on passengers and goods etc.

(3) Taxes levied and collected by the center and compulsorily distributed between the Union and the States (Article 270), Example: taxes on income other than agricultural income.

(4) Taxes levied and collected by the center and may be distributed between the Union and the states, if Parliament by law so provide (Article 272), Example: Union excise duties etc.

(5) Taxes levied and collected and retained by the Center. Example: customs, corporation tax etc.

(b) Item of State List

The state governments can levy, collect and appropriate taxes from land revenue, agricultural incomes, sales and purchase taxes, taxes on consumption and sale of electricity, taxes on vehicles etc.

(c) Other Financial Resources

(1) Article 275 empowers Parliament to give financial assistance to the States in need of such assistance. These grants are based upon the recommendation of Finance Commission.

(2) Article 282 empowers the center to make public purpose grants to the states and to any institution within the states.

(3) Article 293 provides that States can take loan for any purpose.

The grants and loans covered under Articles 282 and 293 are discretionary, therefore they are outside the purview of Finance Commission, An important development in India's fiscal federalism is the emergence of "transfers", before Gadgil Formula of 1969. There was no such formula which dealt with the matters of "transfer". Under Gadgil Formula, the centrally sponsored schemes were given the preference.[10] So, there is an erosion of state's fiscal autonomy through excessive Center's interventions.

India's fiscal federal institution uses a political and economic perspective for the working of a federal system. India's size, density, institutional complexity, regional political competition, political bargaining, etc., compel its fiscal federalism to have its roots in regional political and economic diversity. Many Indian states are quite large and some have largest density in population. Therefore, Indian fiscal and federal structures have no other alternative rather than taking into account these non-fiscal dimensions into consideration while drafting the federal fiscal policies.

Economic Disparity in India

As the wealth of constituent units within a federation (here referring to Indian federation) differs greatly, so it's affects their ability to raise own-source revenues. Thus like other federations, India also have to deal with these economic regional differences therefore it provide provisions for greater transfers to poorer constituent units, though almost all constituting units have same responsibilities yet they cannot have the same ability to meet those responsibilities because of their different abilities to raise required revenues.[11] This unequal treatment brought the concept of economic disparity which also have implication towards social, regional and political disparities.

The constituent units of a federal polity in principles enjoy equal political authority and parity in their relations with national government but when this same principles of authority and parity is related to economy then automatically the issues of unequal size, resource endowment[12] etc., come into being which brings inequality on economic terms. Thus, the problem of disparity is major concern for any federations and the same is valid for India. In Indian context, economic disparity is in the areas of natural resources, economic growth and fiscal transfers. Due to economic disparities India is a "union of unequal states". This unequal status is not only because of size and population but primarily because of their slackness of autonomy and sovereignty especially in economic matters. Consequently, various states face economic deficits, *i.e.*, difference between expenditure and receipts. Thus the federal system always tries to reduce the imbalance through periodic review, observing functional separations, abolishing discretionary federal fiscal transfers etc. Thus, what distinguishes federalism from general decentralisation is the assignment of inextinguishable powers to sub-national governments and these assignments include both fiscal and non-fiscal dimensions.

The Third-Tier in Indian Federalism

Susane Hoeber Rudolf and Lloyd Rudolf write "that states are making themselves heard and felt politically and economically more than they ever have." Therefore, there is a spread of multi-level political federalism.[13] Through the 73rd and 74th amendment, a third tier of governance has been created, which provide a framework for elected council in rural and urban areas. These two amendments make local governance an important body *vis-a-vis* the Central and the State governments. The rural and urban local bodies, *i.e.*, the panchayats and the municipalities are recognised as an institution of self-governance. After 73rd and 74th Amendments, therefore holding regular elections under state Election Commissions is must, reservation of SC's/ST's and women etc., are some of the mandatory and obligatory functions. Even devolution of financial resources to these bodies are ensured by State Finance Commission, who make recommendations on sharing and assignment of various taxes, duties, toils, etc., and also decide on the grant-in-aid which is to be given to these bodies from the consolidated funds of the states (Fig. 2.1). These provisions

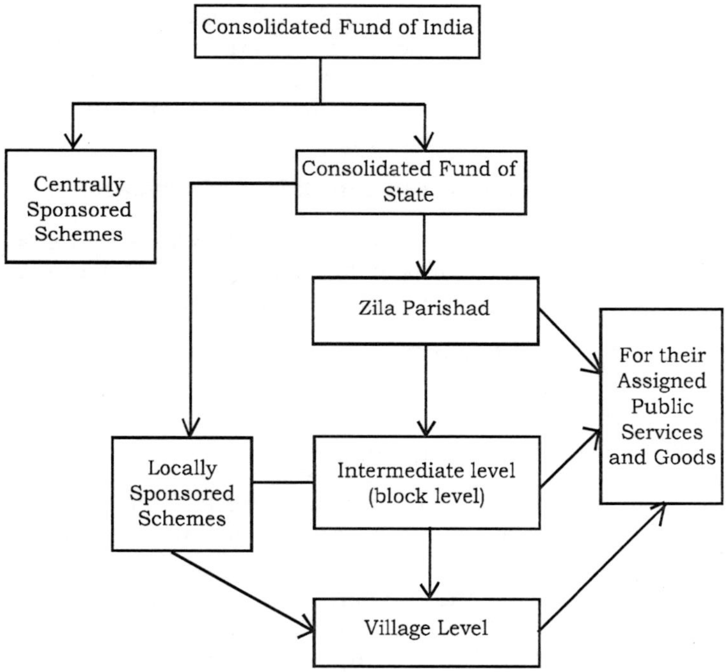

Fig. 2.1. Federal Financial Assignments to the Three Tiers of Government.

are closely related to article 243G and 243W of the constitution.[14]

Fiscal decentralisation to rural local government in India is meaningful only when the Panchayats have adequate untied funds to provide public services assigned to them which require the assignment of tax powers, *i.e.*, the panchayats should be able to raise tax and non-tax revenues from the sources assigned to them or higher level of governments should provide unconditional transfers by way of sharing the taxes or block grants.[15] But the problem is several times inadequate assignments and low-level of efforts are being made in transferring the revenues at the local level governments, therefore the syndrome of fiscal dependency continues. Though sometimes, the State governments undertake certain systematic policy of decentralised planning and administration in the sectors assigned to them but when the same political and bureaucratic forces are used by the center, then it distorts the state-local governmental relations.

Fiscal Imbalances Between the Orders of Governments

The fiscal system has several important inter-linkages between the various organs of the governments. At both the layers of government, the public sector comprises of:

(i) Government departments,

(ii) Departmental enterprises,

(iii) Non-departmental enterpises.[16]

Resources are raised and transferred by each of these organisations from the resources of Central government budget, some are transferred to the state governments and some to the departmental and non-departmental enterprises. Similarly, from the resources of state governments some are transferred to State Public Enterprises and local authorities (on the basis of 73rd and 74th amendments). But when these transfers are not carried in accordance, *i.e.*, by maintaining the required balance, then a situation of fiscal imbalance prevails.

The term "fiscal imbalance" refers to the mis-match between revenue raising capacity and expenditure needs at different governmental units.[17] The fiscal imbalances are primarily of two types:

(i) *Vertical Imbalance:* The imbalance at different levels of governments (inter-governmental) are known as "vertical fiscal" imbalances.

(ii) *Horizontal Imbalance:* The imbalances at different units of same level of governmental (inter-jurisdictional) are known as "horizontal fiscal" imbalances.

Division of powers among different governmental units vertically between different levels of government and horizontally between different jurisdictions with each level is the starting point of examination of efficiency in the delivery of public services. The problems of spillovers, disharmony, and imbalances have their roots in the assignment of finances to various bodies.[18] Therefore the major responsibility of the central government is:

(i) To provide public and merit goods and services, that means centra) government should play an important role in macroeconomic stabilisation, poverty alleviation etc.

(ii) And also to monitor the inter-jurisdictional competition present between Sub-Central governmental units, i.e., to secure a stability in horizontal competition.

Vertical Fiscal Imbalances

No federalism is indifferent of having vertical fiscal imbalances, that is the case with Indian federal structure also. As many-a-times the central government has more comparative advantage in raising the revenues in comparison to state governments, therefore it leads to vertical fiscal imbalances. For example, in India the revenue of central governments flows to state governments in segments and further devolution takes place in the state-level which ultimately flows to the local governments.

Vertical fiscal imbalances can also cause by factors other than assignments. At sub-national levels, inter-governmental tax competition can result in lower tax rates. Therefore vertical fiscal imbalance essentially leads to fiscal dependence of sub-national governments on the central governments.

Horizontal Fiscal Imbalance

Horizontal fiscal imbalances refer to the mismatch present between revenues and expenditure of governmental units within a level of governments. As the states in Indian suffers from hetrogenity in economic and fiscal terms, therefore horizontal fiscal imbalances often take place. In terms of economics, the horizontal equity criteria is, the two persons (states) equally well of before the introduction of the fiscal system should also be so afterwards.[19] It is in the light of this criteria/understanding, we have to see how horizontal imbalances in India exists and what fiscal policies are in place. In India, there are vast differences in per capita, revenue and expenditure, states domestic products as well as in other physical infrastructure and also in terms of natural resources like mines and minerals and geographical/ locational differences. These differences create vast gap between level of investment required to bring some form of developmental leverage to the less developed states with that of more developed states in India. It is equally worth pointing out that even among the developed states, there are "differences" even among themselves in various spheres of economic, geographical and political outlook.

For tackling this issue of horizontal imbalance, in India, the states have been divided into 2 categories:[20]

1. *Special States:* Those states which require special attention, in terms of economic inputs to overcome their imbalances. Example: seven North-eastern states, Sikkim, Jammu and Kashmir, Himachal Pradesh, Uttaranchal. These states primarily suffer imbalances because of their infavourable geographical locations coupled with other factors like strategic locations, ethnicity etc. The special states receive their allocation of fund in the form of 90 per cent grant (i.e., non-refundable) and remaining 10 per cent only as loan(which is refundable).

2. *Non-Special States:* those states which need money but doesn't require special treatment like special states,

in terms of economic help/assistance. Example: Maharashtra, Punjab, Tamil Nadu, West Bengal etc. By and large 70 per cent financial assistance from Center is received in the form of Loan (which is refundable) by the Non-Special states. The remaining thirty per cent comes to Non-Special states/as grants (which is non-refundable).

Sometimes apart from locational/geographical disadvantages, man made differences were also put into place by design or by default. For example: Digboi in Assam has oldest oil field in the country but no steps were taken still recent times to get any LPG unit or ancillary unit of petroleum products in Assam. The crude oil was used to be transported through pipes over more than thousand kilometers in UP for refining. Therefore Assam suffered from such non-implementation/non-planning of these industries relating to crude oil.

Debt Profile of States in 2002-03

State	*Debt to GSDP ratio (per cent)*	*Share in total debt of States (per cent)*	*Range of ratio of interest payment to revenue receipts (per cent)*
(1)	*(2)*	*(3)*	*(4)*
Andhra Pradesh	28.85	7.5	22.28
Bihar	55.33	4.79	22.28
Chhatisgarh	25.46	1.2	10.18
Goa	28.15	0.46	18.22
Gujarat	33.93	6.61	22,29
Haryana	27.86	2,7	22.28
Jharkhand	24.28	1.29	18.22
Karnataka	25.12	4.72	18.22
Kerala	36.34	4.66	22.28
Madhya Pradesh	32.26	4.07	18.22

(Contd...)

(Contd...)

(1)	(2)	(3)	(4)
Maharashtra	21.58	9.51	18.22
Orissa	52.03	4.23	>35
Punjab	48.51	5.52	>35
Rajasthan	45.38	6.31	28.35
Tamil Nadu	26.9	6.02	18.22
Uttar Pradesh	30.08	11.9	28.35
West Bengal	41.15	10.46	>35
Special Category States			
Arunachal Pradesh	55.45	0.18	10.18
Assam	33.91	1.94	10.18
Himachal Pradesh	63.25	1.71	28.35
Jammu and Kashmir	53.8	1.86	10.18
Manipur	43.09	0.31	10.18
Meghalaya	22.17	0.22	10.18
Mizoram	91.56	0.27	10.18
Nagaland	52.1	0.38	10.18
Sikkim	60.27	0.13	10.18
Tripura	37.78	0.46	10.18
Uttaranchal	22.37	0.8	10.18

Of late, situation have been changing and many economic packages are being given to these states in addition to normal plan assistance of the Center. These are some of the examples of fiscal imbalances which are being addressed by different policy measures including fiscal correctives through different mechanisms.

Federal Fiscal Corrective and Mechanisms

Due to the existence of vertical and/or horizontal federal fiscal imbalances, fiscal dependence of the recipient governments on the other layer of the government increased tremendously. And thus the dimension of states fiscal autonomy becomes an important element of federal fiscal structure. In the Indian context fiscal imbalance exists in the form of division of tax power and functions between the center and the states (vertical imbalances) and it exists also due to difference in the endowment position of certain resources of the states (horizontal imbalances). And even in the India context erosion and reduction of fiscal imbalance and dependency is possible only by having more fiscal autonomy and more fiscal flexibility.[21]

In reference with above discussions, I think all federation face a particular challenge, *i.e.,* the wealth of constituent units differs greatly, therefore it affects their ability, to raise own-source revenues. Thus all federations have some provisions for dealing with these differences and imbalances by adopting such provisions which allow greater transfers to poorer constituent units.[22] The federal governments tries to provide programmes of equalisation to overcome the fiscal imbalances. And that is why the Inter-State Council (ISC) came into existence. The ISC is thus supposed to be an effective mechanism to have discussion on crucial economic and social concerns in the country and to know what are the pulses of the state governments on those issues.

Problems and Emerging Challenges in Federal Finance

Under this heading I will discuss, some of the major challenges and problems present within the system of federal finance, which ultimately result in fiscal imbalances. Therefore it is necessary to locate these problems and challenges, so that some correctives are applied to remove the fiscal imbalances. Though, at the cost of some repetition being made here (in reference with earlier position), yet it is useful to have an overall outlook of what kinds of problems and challenges exist in the federal fiscal system in India:

(1) *A Centralised Federation in terms of Distribution of Functions:* In India, it is the constitution which has distributed the powers and functions of central and a state governments. But the circumstances in which India adopted a federal form of government was full of regional

disparities, historical differences, cultural diversity, the problems of princly states etc. which compelled India to have a centralised form of federal system in terms of appointment of the governor, all India administrative services, emergency etc. These mechanism enable the central government to exercise its influence and control over the states.[23]

(2) *Tax Powers:* Though there is a provision for co-equal role for the central as well as for the state governments yet in practice the most broad-based and progressive tax powers are assigned to the center. The important central taxes are customs, excise duty on manufactured goods, income tax etc. The state government also have a few tax bases assigned to them, the power to levy retail sales tax is the most important.

(3) *Tax Sharing:* The concept of tax-sharing is that the rates are entirely dependant upon the discreation of the layer who imposes it, only the proceeds are shared by the other layers of government. And, as the central government has more powers as far as tax power is concerned, therefore the state governments infact have no say on the decisions of the central government.

(4) *Relation with Local Self-Government:* Many-a-times the central government wants to have direct financial contacts with the local government (at rural and urban level) and thus problem arises, as the local governments comes under the preview of state governments, therefore state governments want that they should directly deal with local governments on the matter of finance and central government should provide fund to the state government rather than to the local levels divertly.

(5) *Conditional Grants:* The division of the functions between the center and the states remain logical and apt so far the division does not curb or encroach the independence of the state governments. But, as per the Indian Constitution, it is the central government which has power to raise more funds and later allocates them to the states, therefore a serious problem is often faced by the state

government, *i.e.,* some times the state government has no other alternative rather than to accept the "conditions"[24] imposed by the central governments while giving a particular grant to the state governments for performing their (state governments) tasks and duties.

(6) *Making 'Paul States':* Another problematic area of fiscal federalism is transfer of wealth from one category of states to other states, *i.e.,* fiscal federalism involves the transfer of hard-earned prosperity from states that are more productive, diligent and thrifty to those that are not. G.Ramachandra calls this particular outlook of fiscal federalism as "Rob-Peter-to-pay-Paul approach." But in India there are very few states that are wealthy enough to be robbed. However, a feeling persists that even those "comparatively wealthy" states are being robbed to give wealth to poorer ones. According to Ramachandran, the main problem in this approach is that often the productive states are punished of being wealthy as their wealth is transferred to the poor states who may need the finance but who are not performing week even within their limited scope. Therefore all states become poorer.[25]

(7) *Macro Economy:* Another problematic area of fiscal federalism is that, the central government is primarily concerned with macro economic stability and thus many-a-times ignore the socio-economic reality at the sub level of governance.[26] Since it is the state governments who are primarily responsible for taking care of the quality of life of the ordinary citizen, thus state governments are handicapped in these situations as the focus of the central government is to stick to macro-economic considerations only.

Fiscal Correctives

In India as is known that there are three major channels devolution of various taxes and receipts by the respective governments namely the:

(i) Central Finance Commission appointed by Government of India, for deciding the size of the amount that is to be

transferred from Central kitty and it also decides about the manner and the quantum that is to be given to various states (special and non-special states as it is mentioned under Section III, under the heading of Horizontal fiscal imbalances).

(ii) State Level Finance Commission for the similar tasks as of the Central Commission but in the field of transfers from state kitty to local bodies (rural and urban level), and

(iii) The Planning Commission which plays a key role about deciding the plan size of respective states, depending upon the resources of the states *vis-a-vis* the amount of central grant to be given as Central Plan Assistance (CPA) or Special Central Plan Assistance (SCPA) or through Centrally Sponsored Schemes (CSS).

In addition to this, various ministries also give grants to their counterparts in the states for specified programmes, either wholly funded by the Center (central sector projects) or requiring the states to share a proportion of the cost (Centrally Sponsored Schemes). Thus we find that the most important characteristics of Indian federal fiscal arrangements is the existence of multiple channels for "center-state transfers". These fiscal arrangements offers a transparent platform to the center, states and also to the civil society in many cases to participate during the process of Central Finance Commission hearings in various states and Planning Commission meetings with different states from time to time. These transparent arrangements act as a "check and balance" to overcome any biasness on the part of a higher governance authority in sharing their proceeds with the next governance channels. Thus the present arrangement is taking into account the needs of various states *vis-a-vis* their weaknesses and strong points in asking share from central kitty, state kitty, as the case may be.

The Finance Commission (Central and State Level)

The Finance Commission was envisaged in the constitution as the key institution responsible for dealing with fiscal federal imbalances present between the central government and state government. Act 280 of the constitution provide the provision of a Finance Commission (at five year intervals) to recommend the President on the matters related to financial resources.[27] Both, the high-level Apex Finance Commission (AFC) and the State Finance Commission (SFC's) are constitutionally enstructed with the role of supervising the economic systems and parameters and even modified them as needed. The major duty of the Commission is to make recommendations to the President on the issues[28]:

(i) Distribution of taxes between the central government and state governments.

(ii) On which principles the grant-in-aid is given to the state governments from the Consolidated Fund of India.

(iii) What measures should be needed to augment the Consolidated Fund of the State, to supplement the resources of the Panchayat and Municipalities in the state.

(iv) Any other matter that are also referred to by the President in the interest of sound finance.

Apart from these basic exercise, the AFC also under takes the following functions:[29]

(i) awards some compensatory grants,

(ii) awards grants for specific purpose at its discretion,

(iii) give advices on fiscal mechanisms for calamity relief,

(iv) also give advices on necessary measures with regard to state indebtedness to the central authority.

Table 2.1

Sl. No.	*Year of Finance Commission*	*Recommendations*
1.	1st Finance Commission was constituted in 1951	55 per cent of the net proceeds of income tax should be distributed among the states.
2.	5th Finance Commission was constituted in 1968	The state share of income-tax should be raised to 75 per cent and the Unions exercise duty should be raised to 20 per cent.
3.	6th Finance Commission was constituted in 1973	The commission, for the first time looked into the debt position of the states.
4.	8th Finance Commission was constituted in 1982	Recommended various grants of money to the states.
5.	10th Finance Commission was constituted in 1992	Public sector units were given sufficient importance and thus GDP increased upto 9.46 per cent.
6.	11th Finance Commission was constituted in 1998	Control over consumption expenditure and subsidies and also recommend for the improvement of resource mobilising capacity of PSU's both at the central and at the state levels.
7.	12th Finance Commission was constituted in 2005-06 and it is still continuing.	Still now 60 per cent of total transfer have been made and in addition the central ministries also give specific purpose transfers to states with or without matching requirements.
8.	13th Finance Commission 2007	Working.

Some of the major recommendations made by the various Finance Commission are:

The Planning Commission

The Planning Commission is a major dispenser of funds to the State.[30] It is an extra-constitutional and non-statutory body, which was set up on the resolution of Union Cabinet by the first Prime Minister Jawahar Lal Nehru, to formulate an integrated 5 year plan, for economic and social development. It acts as an advisory body. The Planning Commission transfers are primarily for "developmental purpose" including "project specific expenditure" also. This formula involves a complex balancing objectives, *i.e.*, to maintain, vertical and horizontal equity at the same time meeting needs of different states.

The working of Planning Commission led to the setting up of another extra-constitutional and extra-legal body, namely NATIONAL DEVELOPMENT COUNCIL (NDC) in 1952. The main task of the council is to associate the states in the formulation of the Plans, to ensure a balanced and rapid development in all parts of the country (both at Central and State level). The NDC though an extra-constitutional body yet it facilitate a dialogue sharing process towards formulation of five year plan of the country by the Planning Commission.

Though many critics are of the opinion that Planning Commission is a body which encroach upon the autonomy of the states under the federal system. But the justification for setting up of Planning Commission is that, it is that body which help in the financing of the states in a formula based manner. The Planning Commission coupled with Finance Commission through their functioning make the fiscal federal system more apt and healthy in nature for both the central government and for the state and local governments.

Sarkaria Commission

The recommendations of the Sarkaria Commission with respect to financial relations between the union and the states constitute the most important part of all recommendations. This commission was set up primarily to revise the center-state relationship.[31] On financial matters, the main aim of this commission was to maintain a balance between two levels of governments. Therefore the commission has taken favourable view on the demand of the states to have more financial resources at their disposal, *i.e.,* the commission introduced those effective measures which are more decentralised in nature. Some of the important recommendation of fiscal federal given by Sarkaria Commission are:[32]

(i) More resource devolution for the states.

(ii) Maintaining strict financial discipline on part of the Union as well as of the states.

(iii) The Finance Commission's division should be in cooperation with state governments.

(iv) Adequate flow of funds to the backward regions.

To sum up Sarkaria Commission's role, one may say that it is that body which helped in connecting the Finance Commission with Planning Commission and it also not only dealt with on financial issues but also on issues like legislative and administrative matters, which in aggregate sense led to strengthening of federal roots future in India. Recently, a new Commission has been set up under the Chairmanship of Justice Punch, to go into further in the matters of Central State relationship in the post-development of Sarkaria Commission.

Why We Need Fiscal Correctives?

Fiscal policy is the building block for an enabling macro-environment, which not only provides stability and predictability to the policy regime, but through its tax transfer mechanism, it also ensures that national resources are allocated in terms of its defined priorities.[33] The fiscal imbalance was identified as the root cause of the twin problems of the inflation and the difficult balance of payments position. Therefore, a strong institutional mechanism is required to overcome the fiscal imbalance deficit. Towards this end, enactment of FISCAL REFORMS AND BUDGET MANAGEMENT ACT (FRBMA) is the important institutional expression which ensure fiscal prudence and also support macro-economic balance. FRBMA provides the basic structure around which many fiscal measures have been implemented. These measures include:[34]

(i) Reducing peak rates of customs duties;

(ii) Rationalising excise duties;

(iii) Introduction of state level tax;

(iv) Introduction of innovative financing mechanism like; creation of Special Purpose Vehicles (SPV).

Reform of India's Fiscal Federal Institutions

Tax Reform after 1990 includes reduction of tariff rates, reduction in direct tax rates couples with attempts to broaden the tax base and a gradual movement from excise duties and sales taxes to a Value Added Tax (VAT) by both the Central and State Governments.[35]

Thus the need for making reforms and fiscal system has gone beyond the central finance (i.e., Finance Commission, Planning Commission and other Central measures). As has been stated earlier the sale tax and the state exercise are the most important source of revenue for the states. The divergent rate structure under sale tax of the states was so complex and contradictory that one states sale tax policy used to effect adversary. The other states ability to collect sale tax. In the interest of fiscal discipline and bringing a harmonised sale tax system in each of the states without disturbing the autonomy of the states to impose sale tax and collect revenues, a high powered expert committee under the Chairmanship of Prof. Ashim Dasgupta (Finance Minister, West Bengal) was set up. Through an elaborative Consultancy process, this committee suggested for introduction of VAT in place of sale tax. This was a great sale tax reform for a big federal state like India. This VAT is an improve system of irnposion of sale tax and its collections through reduction in the tax rates and its harmonisation. All the state excepting UP had accepted VAT since two years. Now the state of UP has also joined. This reform in sale tax structure indicates how important for a federal country like India to adopt fiscal correctives through a consultative process rather than infusing from the Center.

Similar exercise is been undertaken for imposition of a consolidate goods and service tax, for the entire county in place of difference good and services tax. This is being target by 2010. Thus FRBM, VAT and Consolidate goods and services tax would make the foundation of fiscal federalism much stronger in India and the beauty is that all such reforms are being undertaken through a dialogue between the Union and the states and also among the states. All in all these are examples of sound fiscal correctives in a federalism.

According to Dr M. Govind Rao, we need fiscal corrective because Indian federalism is moving from a situation where the Centre distributed its surpluses to the States in spite of there is a deficits gap in the process of distribution. Thus, financial federalism has been dominated by both vertical and horizontal inequity which is not only leads to fiscal crisis (basically on states part) but it also leads to the rise of unresolved conflicts. So, unless we formulate a certain kind of effective and durable corrective measures in the fiscal system itself, we can't have an effective devolution of authority from Center to the States in the form of policy and planning decentralisation. To achieve desired goal, we must take some major changes required in the area of fiscal policy.[36] These are:

1. Changes in the financing pattern of the fiscal deficits by reducing dependence on the system of monetising the deficit.
2. Changes in expenditure pattern through reduced transfer payments.
3. Budgetary support to Public Sector Policy (PSP) is very important.

References

1. Julia Darby, Anton Muscatelli and Graeme Roy, *Federalism and fiscal autonomy–Lessons for the UK from other industrialised countries,* www.gla.ac.uk/media-22250-en.pdf.
2. The idea of asymmetrical federalism is some members may be less equal and thus enjoy a lower degree of autonomy because special circumstances. Example J&K in India.
3. *The Indian Express*–March 10, 2008.
4. See www.gla.ac.uk/media-22250-en.pdf.
5. Ashok Kumar Chada, *Federalism in India: A study of union-state relations,* pp. 185—186.
6. *Ibid.,* pp. 187—188.
7. D.D. Basu, *Introduction to Indian Constitution,* pp. 322—324.
8. *Ibid.,* p. 325.
9. B.L. Fadia, *Indian Government and Politics,* pp.
10. Managing fiscal federalism; revenue allocation issues, publics, pp. 103—111.
11. G. Anderson, *Federalism: An introduction,* pp. 5,8.
12. Ajit Mazumdar, pp. 40—45.
13. Akhtar Majeed, India's Extreme Diversity Makes Pluralism Imperative, www.forumfed.org/libdocs/Federations/V7N1e_in_Majeed.pdf
14. More plans of Panchayats and Municipalities are incorporated under 11th and 12th scheduled of the Indian Constitution.
15. See more in www.forumfed.org/libdocs/Federations/V7N1e_in_Majeed.pdf.

16. See more in www.forumfed.org/libdocs/Federations/V7N1e_in_Majeed.pdf
17. G. Anderson, pp. 5—6.
18. Ajit Mazumdar, pp. 8—10.
19. *Ibid.*, pp. 11—15.
20. There is a great variation in the design and underlying principles for such transfers.
21. J. Copland, Federalism, pp. 5—6.
22. D.D. Basu, pp. 51—61.
23. *Ibid.*, pp. 56—57.
24. G. Ramachandran, *Fiscal federalism: Making 'Paul states'*, www.thehindubusinessline.com/todays-paper/tp-opinion*article2179874.ece.
25. www.thehindubusinessline.com/todays-paper/tp-opinion*article2179874.ece.
26. The State Government deals with the provision of sanitation facilities, health, education etc.
27. D.D. Basu, pp. 57—61.
28. *Ibid.*, pp. 329—330.
29. Ajit Mazumdar, pp. 40—41.
30. D.D. Basu, pp. 326—327.
31. B.L. Fadia, pp. 249—250.
32. *Ibid.*, pp. 249—253.
33. *Ibid.*, pp. 250—251.
34. The Eleventh Five Year Plan (2007—12), Government of India, Planning Commission.
35. Ajit Mazumdar, pp. 70—75.
36. *Ibid.*, pp. 70—71.

3 A Comparative Study of Indian Fiscal Federalism with Canadian and Australian Fiscal Federalism

As allocation of financial resources is one of the most crucial subjects of interest in federalism, so federal and non-federal countries are concerned about what type of federal-fiscal system should they have? This is because federalism is not only about division of powers between the Central and the State government rather it (federalism) is a mechanism also, which can bring a balanced relationship between different layers of government and this balancing relationship is only possible if there is a good cooperation and coordination between the levels of governments on the aspects of administrative as well as financial matters.

The main objective of making a comparison between Indian fiscal federalism with the Canadian and the Australian fiscal federalism are that they have different understanding of practicing the concept as their method of fiscal federalism and its applicability are also different to some extent despite they have adopted the common Westmin ster-style of parliamentary system.[1]

Different Perception of Federalism

Indian federal structure is very close to Canadian structure. India adopted the federal model of governance from the Canadian federal system. Both India and Canada have almost the same kind of federalism in the context of cultural in nature. But on the other hand, Australia is a clear case of territorial federalism.[2] The concept of the Australian federalism is not only to accommodate cultural differences but also to accommodate various inter regional differences *i.e.,* various regions must have common advantages *vis-a-vis* the Central Governments.

In true sense, the parliamentary-federal system in Canada and in India are on the basis of "centralised governance" still both these countries believed in the idea of "share-rule" in a federal system. In constrast, the Australian federal structure gives much more attention towards the needs of state or to some extent supports "self-rule" system.[3]

Another important difference between these three federal countries is that, in India and in Canada the residency power rests with the central government but India unlike Canada give more emphasis on the concurrent list where both the Central and State government have powers and work in a tandem for a common goal. On the other hand, the 'residual' powers in Australia stays with the States. In that context, if we take the things in right perspective, the relationship between the Central Government and the State government is not same in these three federal countries.

Australia and Canada have dual federalism where the local government are the hand maiden of state governments and it is the federal governments which directly deals with the local governments but in India we have three tiers/order of government and it is the State governments which is soley responsible in executing the powers and decides the policy matters in view of smooth running of the local governments functions.

How India, Canada and Australia Looks into the Concept of Fiscal Federalism?

Federal countries differ a great deal in their choices as to the character of fiscal federalism, specifically, how the division of fiscal powers are allocated among various layers of the governments and what kind of fiscal arrangements should be that have to be decided by the federal countries. Despite of having different perceptions about the fiscal federal system all these three countries—India, Canada and Australia, broadly (as per their respective Constitution) divided the area or powers of the Central government and various the State governments in more or less in the same pattern. In all the three countries the Central government have powers in running the functioning of defence, foreign affairs, international trade, and customs etc., whereas the State governments primarily deal with the portfolios of health, education, and public services etc.[4]

Following are the basic differences can be observed in these three federal countries as far as their fiscal-federal system is concerned:

1. In India, the provision of generating resources through the income tax has remained exclusively with federal government, therefore it is the federal government which is empowered to provide various grants to the constituency units. But no such specific federal-fiscal power is mentioned in the Australia and in the Canadian Constitution.

2. Most federation have the arrangements for correcting the vertical and horizontal financial imbalances which are present in either different level of government or present within a particular level of government respectively. The point of difference is that India and Australia is concerned particularly for the removable of both vertical and horizontal imbalances but Canada on the other hand is more focused on the rectifying the horizontal imbalance present in its federal-fiscal system.[5]

3. The primary task of fiscal-federal system is to deals with the imbalances present between the different layers of governments. For these, India and Australia both have appointed expert commissions for determining the distributive formulae between the Central and State governments. But Canada on the other hand believes in more "equalisation" scheme. Therefore, there is limited scope of tax competition amongst the Canadian provinces.[6]

4. Economic and regional disparities are the most common problems faced by all the federal countries

> like India, Canada and Australia. These three federal countries adopted "formula based approach" for reducing the disparities.[7] But Canada and India have a complex set of formulae in order to understand and meeting the inequalities presents in the States. Canada unlike India always has a target of achieving equalisation goals. Australia, on the other hand, followed a least' complex formula-based approach, therefore, Australia gives more autonomy to the states. Here, in the context of Canada and India try to help the more backward provinces and states to achieve economic parity. Therefore, the Canadian and the Indian federalism face more controversies in the spheres of the socio-economic and political at the time of handling fiscal federalism *vis-a-vis* Australia.

On the basis of above discussions, here is a table given which clearly defines the similarities and dissimilarities present between these thrre federal countries (India, Canada and Australia) on fiscal federalism concept.

Table 3.1

SN	*Fiscal Issues*	*India*	*Canada*	*Australia*
1.	Central government's transfer relative to constituent-unit spending.	Central government is the largest funders of state *i.e.*, upto 46 percent they transfer.	Smallest central transfer i.e., 13 to 26percent.	Same with that of India, the central government give the largest share up 46percent.
2.	Legal provisions around spending power in federation.	The grants of central governments is more important aspect of jurisdiction.	Court interpretation matters the most.	Central government have the jurisdictional authority.
3.	Fiscal imbalances.	Both vertical and horizontal imbalances present. The issue of income tax solely belongs to the central authority, therefore more heterogeneity present between the states and central government.	Horizontal imbalance more dangerous than the vertical imbalance.	Though both vertical and horizontal imbalances exist but in Australia, the vertical imbalance is too large than the horizontal one.
4.	Income tax	Weak	Income tax system is harmonised as the provinces have longer responsibility for raising their revenues.	Same like India.
5.	Equalising-fiscal capacity	Yes	Yes	Yes
6.	Adjusting expenditure needs.	Combining the national, state and local level government.	No	Yes
7.	Economic data is based on	Finance commission and planning commission.	Only central and state level government plays in important role.	Like India 3 tier exists.
8.	Grant administration.		Department of finance.	Grant commissions.

References

1. T.O. Hueglin, *Comparative Federalism: A Systematic Inquiry,* pp. 20— 30.
2. *Ibid.,* pp. 20—25.
3. *Ibid.,* pp. 14—16.
4. Balver Arora and Varney, pp. 100—101.
5. Jay Makarenko, *Federalism in Canada: Basic Framework and Operation,* www.mapleof web.com/ features/federalism-Canada-basic-framework-and-operation.
6. www.mapleof web.com/features/federalism-Canada-basic-framework-and-operation.
7. www.mapleof web.com/features/federalism-Canada-basic-framework-and-operation.

Conclusion

The analysis of federalism in Indian context is broadened beyond a narrow constitutional-legal framework. The Indian federalism is an experience which revolves around the following themes like diversity, fiscal federalism, local government as a three-tier of government and inter-governmental relations.[1] In this paper, under various sections, an attempt has been made to show that federal countries have a remarkable ability to adapt and to meet the emerging challenges of fiscal federalism in the face of economic disparities and other non-economic factors, (in this paper, a detailed case study of India has been discussed in section IV, and compared Indian fiscal-federalism with the Austrialian and Canadian fiscal federalism). Though there are many difficult challenges are observed in all the federal countries. Especially in the context of India which wanted to have a cooperative federalism rather than a competitive one.

Competition and cooperation are often overlapping facts of Indian federal system. The thrust of the concept of cooperative federalism grew basically as a critiqtie of the static two-tier governments. Cooperative federalism is that the form of federalism which though produces a strong Central government yet it doesnot necessarily results in weaking provincial governments.[2]

Therefore, James Bryce and Prof K.C. wheare argue that federalism is that system of government in which both the Central government and the regional government coordinate and cooperate with each other independently.[3]

And this cooperation and coordination is not only restricted to political claims but it (cooperation and coordination) should be in economic matters also. The fiscal federalism is thus, important not only because that it allows economic devolution (each tiers of governments have sufficient financial autonomy to carry their assigned work) but it is also facilitates and strengthen political federalism by addressing the economic disparity in a larger perspective. That is to say that unless fiscal federalism is followed in right earnest, the political federalism will get diluted or distorted and the federal character of a country will suffer.

References

1. D.D. Basu, p. 60.

2. Federalism should increase the state autonomy and also it should increase the activation of local Governments.

3. Federalism without a Centre.

Bibliography

Anderson, George (2007), Real Federalism: A system that adopts to *countries needs,* Federation Vol. 6th Feb./March.

......(2007), *What India can show the world,* Federalism, Oct./Nov.

......(2008), *Federalism : An Introduction,* Oxford University Press.

Arora Balveer and Douglas V. Varney (1995), *Multiple identities in a single state: Indian Federalism in Comparative Perspectives,* Konark Publishers Pvt. Ltd.

......(1995), *Adapting Federalism to India: Multilevel and Asysmetrical Innovations.*

......and Nirmal Mukharji, *Restructuring Federal Democracy.*

Basu, D.D. (2005), *Introduction to the Constitution of India,* Wadhwa Publishers.

Bird, Richard M *Fifcal Federalism,* University of Toronto.

Boadway, Robin (2007), *Canada: Emerging issue in a Decentralised Federation* (A global Dialogue of Federalism) Vol. 4.

Bose, Taun Chandra (1987), *Indian Federalism Problems and fsmuefi,* K.P. Bagchi and Publishers.

Brito, Camargo and Ricardo (2006), *The Globalisation debate, revisited : of the constraints of fiscal policies of the nation state.*

Compland lan and John Rickard (2001), Federalism: *Comparative Perspectives from India and Australia,* Mohan Pub. ND-02.

Fadia, B.L. (2005), *Indian Government and Politics,* Sathiya Bhawan Publication.

Ghosh, Jayati (2005), *The death of Fiscal Federalism?* THE HINDU, June, 07.

Gupta, U.N. (1988), *Indian Federalism and Unity of Nation: A Review of Indian Constitutional Experiences,* Vohra Pub. and distributors.

Grewal, Bhajan S. (2001), *Federalism and Fiscal Equalisation: Should India follow the Australian Path?* Mohan Pub.

Hueglin T.O. (2007), *Conflict Resolution in Emerging Multilateral World.*

Jayal, Niraja Gopal, Amit Prakash and Pradeep K. Sharrna (2006), *Local Governance in India: Decentralisation and Beyond* Oxford University Press.

Kabbur, A.S. (2004), *Center-State Relation in India: Perception of Non-Congress Political Parties,* Nice Printing Press.

Krishnaswamy, K.S.; I.S. Gulati arid A. Vaidyanathan, *Economic Aspects of Federalism in India.*

Lakdawala, D.T. (1967), Problems in Federal Finance (Union State Financial Relations), Lalvani Pub. house.

Leuprecht, Christian (2007), *The Theory* and *The Practice of Federalism,* Federation, Vol. 6, Feb./March.

Mahajan, Curpreet (2007), *Restructuring the Center—State relationship in India,* Federation, Oct./Nov.

Majeed, Akhtar (2005), *An Introductionto Federalism,* Center for Federal Studies, Hamdard University, New Delhi.

......(2007), India: *The Emergence of Cooperative Federalism.*

......(2007), *India's extreme diversity makes pluralism imperative,* Federation, Oct./Nov.

Massicotte, Louis (2005), *How do federal countries choose their governments?* Federation Vol. 5.

McLean, Lain (2003), *Fiscal Federalism in Canada,* University of Oxford.

Morris, Alan (2007), *Australia: Equity, Imbalance and Equalitarianism,* (A Global Dialogue of Federalism).

Mozoomdar, Ajit (2005), *The Political Economy of Modern Federalism.*

Pandey, Jaya (2003), *Fiscal Federalism in India.*

Parthasarathy, G. (2001), *Federalism and Constitutional Process in India.*

Rao, M. Govinda (2005), *Indian Fiscal Federalism from a Comparative Perspectives.*

......(2007), *Fiscal Federalism and Management.*

......(2007), *Fiscal Federalism in Idnia:Emerging Challenges.*

......and Nirvikar Singh (2007), *The Political Economy of India's Fiscal Federal System and its Reforms,* Publius, Vol. 37, Winter.

.... (2005), *The Political Economy of Federalism in India.*

Rao, M. Govinda (2008), *Republic of India.*

......and U.A. Vasanthn Rao (2008), *Expanding the Resource Base of Panchayats Augmenting Own Revenues,* EPW, 26th Jan.

Rao, D.N. (1998), *Dimension of Federal National Building,* Center for Federal Studies, Jamia Hamdard University.

Rao, Rokkam S. (2001), *Federalism and Fiscal Autonomy of States.* The Indian Experience.

Rao, N.R. (1972), *Union-State Financial Relations in India,* S.S. Wodeya Pub.

Ramachandran G. (2005), *Fiscal Federalism:Making 'Paul' States,* THF HINDU, Jurt 10.

Ray Amol and Mohit Bhattacharya (2003), *Political Theory ideas* and *Institutions,* World Press Pub.

Ray, Bharati (1987), *Center—State Financial Relation in India.*

Rodden, Jonathan (2004), *On the Migration of Fiscal Sovereignty*

Roy, Ash Narain (2004), *How India does it.* Federation, Vol. 4.

Sacz, Lawrence (2002), *Federalism Without A Center,* Sage Publication,

Sarkar, R.C. (1986), *Union-State Relation in India,* National Public House.

Sastri and Reddy (1988), *Center-State Financial Relation.*

Sen, Tapas. K. (2007), *How Public Planning and Finance work in India,* Federation, Vol. 6, Feb./March.

Sengupta, Jayashree, *Economic Reforms, the Role of the State, the Future of Center-State Relations* O.R. Foundation.

Shah, Anwar (2008),: *An Introduction : Principle of Fiscal Federalism.*

......(2007), *Comparative Reflection on Emerging Challenges in Fiscal Federalism.*

Sharma, R. (1967), *Indian Federal Structure,* Central Book Depot.

Simpson, Jeffrey (2006), *Canada's new Conservative government faces restive provinces,* Federation, Vol. 5, March/April.

Singh, M.P. (1998), *Paradigm—Shifts in Canadian and Indian Politics.*

Smith, Jennifer (2005), *Canada:A noisy squabble over offshore oil and equalisation,* Federation Vol. 4, March.

Srinivasan, G. (2006), *Fiscal Transfer to local governments not healthy, The Hindu,* March 29.

Verney, Douglas (2005), *Are all Federation Federals The US, Canada and India.*

Watts, Ronald L. (2005), *Parliamentary Federation: Canada and India.*

Index